★ PLAYING PRO ★
FOOTBALL

Paul Bowker

 Lerner Publications Company ● Minneapolis

Lerner Publications Company
A division of Lerner Publishing Group, Inc.
241 First Avenue North
Minneapolis, MN 55401 USA

For reading levels and more information,
look up this title at www.lernerbooks.com.

Content Consultant: Michael Lehan, six-year NFL veteran

Library of Congress Cataloging-in-Publication Data

Bowker, Paul, 1954-
    Playing pro football / by Paul Bowker.
        pages cm. — (Playing pro sports)
    Includes index.
    ISBN 978-1-4677-3844-6 (lib. bdg. : alk. paper)
    ISBN 978-1-4677-4728-8 (eBook)
    1. Football—Juvenile literature. 2. Professional sports—
Juvenile literature. I. Title.
    GV950.7.B69 2015
    796.332'64—dc23   2013046647

Manufactured in the United States of America
1 – PC – 7/15/14

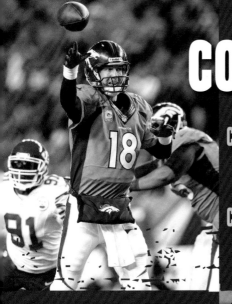

CONTENTS

CHAPTER ONE

FAMILY OF QUARTER

Peyton Manning stepped on the field for his first National Football League (NFL) game during the preseason in 1998. His promise was realized on his first pass. Manning hooked up with wide receiver Marvin Harrison for a 48-yard touchdown.

The play was the start of something big for Manning. He went on to pass for 3,739 yards during his rookie season. He also threw for 26 touchdowns. Then he got even better. Manning's Indianapolis Colts had won just three games in 1998. In 1999 Manning led the team to a 13–3 record. It was the biggest turnaround over two seasons in NFL history. Manning was becoming one of football's all-time best quarterbacks. Great quarterback play in the NFL is a Manning family tradition.

Peyton Manning, opposite page, has proven to be one of the best quarterbacks in NFL history. He joined the Denver Broncos in 2012.

BACKS

Archie Manning is Peyton's father. The New Orleans Saints picked Archie second in the 1971 NFL Draft. He played most of his 13 NFL seasons there. The team often struggled. Yet Archie was one of the bright spots.

Peyton began playing football as a kid with his two brothers. Older brother Cooper Manning was a great wide receiver. He was planning to play at the University of Mississippi like his father. However, health issues ended his college career before he played one game. The younger brothers had no such setbacks. Peyton Manning went on to play at the University of Tennessee. Then the Colts picked him first in the 1998 NFL Draft. Youngest brother Eli Manning played quarterback at Mississippi. In 2004 he too was the top pick in the NFL Draft. Then he led his New York Giants to two Super Bowl victories in his first eight NFL seasons. He was the Super Bowl Most Valuable Player (MVP) both times.

The Manning brothers are gifted athletes. Talent alone does not get a player to

Quotable

"Unbeknownst to the coaches, Cooper and I worked out our own set of signals for that season. We didn't tell anybody except Dad. If I touched my nose, it was a come-back pass [to Cooper, naturally]. Tap my helmet and it was a curl. It wasn't exactly fair to the other receivers, I admit, but they didn't know, and it was working, and we were winning, so we kept doing it. And I can say it now because I know it's true. For a quarterback there's nothing like having your brother as your primary receiver."
—Peyton Manning, on passing to his brother, Cooper Manning, during their games playing for Isidore Newman School of New Orleans

the NFL, though. The NFL Players Association (NFLPA) studied the numbers. It found that approximately 100,000 high school seniors play football each year. Yet only around 215 of them ever make it to the NFL. That is 0.2 percent.

From left: Peyton Manning, Archie Manning, and Eli Manning all became star quarterbacks.

Hall of Famer Red Grange, *center*, poses with two teammates from the 1925 Chicago Bears.

Getting to the NFL is one thing. Staying in the league is a whole other challenge. The NFLPA lists the average NFL career as approximately 3.5 seasons. The best and most consistent players often stay in the league much longer. However, many careers are cut short by injury and ineffectiveness. Athletes such as Peyton and Eli Manning who last for many years in the NFL must dedicate themselves to the sport. After all, football is their full-time job. They must stay fit. They must continue to improve and perform well. And, importantly, they must stay healthy. A badly timed injury or a poor performance can end one's career in an instant. For the players who make it, though, there is nothing quite like playing on Sundays.

At Center Stage

By any measure, the NFL is the most popular sports league in the United States. Stadium seats are usually sold out. NFL games are among the most popular television shows each week. However, it was not always that way.

Football developed on the college level in the late 1800s. The NFL was founded in 1920 as the American Professional Football Association. The league had 14 teams that year. Only the Arizona Cardinals and the Chicago Bears can trace their histories that far back. By 1922 the league had taken on the NFL name. And the Green Bay Packers and the New York Giants were in the NFL by 1925. Still, the league had a long way to go. In fact, the first Super Bowl was not held until January 1967, although the game was not officially called the Super Bowl until Super Bowl III in January 1969.

The Super Bowl became a necessity for the NFL. The NFL was the most popular professional football league.

The Green Bay Packers and the Kansas City Chiefs face off in the 1967 game now known as Super Bowl I.

But the upstart American Football League (AFL) began challenging the NFL in the 1960s. The two leagues soon decided that competing against each other was a bad plan. So the leagues started working together. Each league crowned its own champion. After the 1966 season, the two champions began facing off to determine the ultimate champion. This combined championship game soon became known as the Super Bowl.

The NFL and the AFL officially merged for the 1970 season. The combined league kept the NFL's established name. However, it split the teams into two conferences. Most of the former NFL teams joined the National Football Conference (NFC). The former AFL teams joined the American Football Conference (AFC). The NFC and AFC champions still meet each February in the Super Bowl. Other upstart leagues have since tried to challenge the NFL. None have lasted.

Ready, Set, Throw . . .

Archie, Peyton, Eli, and Cooper Manning partner with a number of college coaches to hold the Manning Passing Academy each year. The summer camp is held at Nicholls State University in Thibodaux, Louisiana. Its creation goes back to 1995. The goal of the Manning Passing Academy is to have a camp where coaches stress the fundamentals of throwing and catching a football. Among the camp's alumni is Andrew Luck. He became Peyton Manning's replacement on the Indianapolis Colts in 2012. Peyton Manning moved on to the Denver Broncos that year. Luck is now a coach at the camp.

The NFL's popularity began to take off after the merger. The first Super Bowl did not even sell out. Over the years, Super Bowl Sunday has become an unofficial holiday. Upwards of 100 million people in the United States watch the game each year. The game is often the most watched television show all year. But even regular-season NFL games have huge popularity. NFL games are routinely the most watched television shows in a given week. In fact, some NFL regular-season games have better television ratings than World Series games.

The NFL's popularity has resulted in high salaries for players. Early NFL players often had to work second jobs during the off-season to make ends meet. The starting salary for a rookie in 2013 was $405,000. Green Bay Packers quarterback Aaron Rodgers was the highest-paid player. He made $22 million that season.

The increased popularity has only made the NFL more competitive, though. More athletes are playing football at all levels. And, modern football players are bigger and stronger than ever. These factors combine to make roster spots even harder to get. There are 32 NFL teams. Each team is allowed to have 53 players during the season. That means there are only 1,696 jobs as an NFL player at a given time. (Eight additional players can join each team's practice squads at lower salaries.) Getting one of those jobs takes a lot more than talent.

IN THE SPOTLIGHT

Being the best in the NFL does not come easily. Minnesota Vikings running back Adrian Peterson is one of the league's top rushers. He suffered a nasty knee injury at the end of the 2011 season. Injuries like his can keep players out of action for a year. But Peterson was back nine months later for the first game of the 2012 season.

The man nicknamed All Day took an intense approach to rehab. Two weeks after surgery, he walked up steps without crutches. He measured his early progress simply by the number of calf raises or knee lifts he could do. In five months, he raced teammate Percy Harvin up a hill during a workout. Then Peterson had one of the best seasons of any running back in NFL history. He rushed for 2,097 yards and 12 touchdowns. He was named the NFL's MVP.

CHAPTER TWO

NFL SKILLS AND

The NFL makes sure incoming players are prepared. One way it does that is through an age limit. Most players enter the league through the NFL Draft. But players must be at least three years removed from high school to be eligible. This rule ensures that the best players have experience on the college level. Players develop physically and mentally during that time. They also prove themselves against good competition. NFL scouts track college games closely.

The NFL is a big-money business. Teams invest millions of dollars into their players. A good selection in the draft can bring a team closer to the Super Bowl. But picking the wrong athletes might mean a losing season. So teams want to make sure they know everything possible about the players. That quest for knowledge is at its peak at the NFL Scouting Combine.

University of Southern California quarterback Matt Leinart tests his vertical leap before the 2006 NFL Draft.

STRENGTH

The combine is a giant event. Approximately 300 NFL Draft prospects attend the four-day event each February. It is usually held in Indianapolis, Indiana. While there, the players undergo a series of physical, psychological, and written tests. The players also interview with team representatives. General managers and scouts from all 32 teams attend the event. Parts of the combine are even shown on television.

University of South Florida defensive end Jason Pierre-Paul goes through an agility drill during a 2010 pro day. The New York Giants selected him in the first round of that year's draft.

What They Are Testing For

Physical tests are at the forefront at the combine. Teams are looking for players who are fast, strong, and agile. So athletes go through tests such as a 40-yard dash to test speed. Various shuttle events test agility. One test involves players bench-pressing 225 pounds (102 kilograms) as many times as possible. Players are also tested for how high they can leap. In addition, players are weighed and measured. Some position-specific drills are also held at the combine. However, many players showcase these skills at pro days too. Pro days are organized workouts for scouts to attend. The workouts usually take place on college campuses. Some players decide to skip the combine in favor of pro days. That option gives the players more time to prepare and more control over the workouts.

Some people question the combine's importance. They note that good scores on physical tests do not necessarily translate to being good football players. The results are mixed. Chris Johnson was a running back from East Carolina University. Most expected him to be taken in the second or third round of the 2008 NFL Draft. But Johnson shined at that year's combine. He ran the 40-yard dash in just 4.24

Fastest Man in the 40

Timing at the NFL Scouting Combine is now done electronically. Chris Johnson's 4.24-second 40-yard dash is the combine record with the new timing system. The unofficial combine record belongs to Bo Jackson. He was clocked at 4.12 seconds by a handheld watch in 1986. Jackson went on to play both pro football and pro baseball. The bigger and heavier offensive linemen also have shown speed. Three offensive linemen turned in times below five seconds at the 2013 combine. Terron Armstead of the University of Arkansas at Pine Bluff topped the list at 4.65 seconds. Many others were under six seconds.

seconds. That tied the all-time combine record. Johnson also performed well in other physical tests. The Tennessee Titans ended up taking Johnson in the first round of the draft. Then, in 2009, he led the NFL with 2,006 rushing yards.

Several other players had the opposite experience, though. Matt Jones was a good quarterback at the University of Arkansas. However, scouts didn't think Jones was good enough to play quarterback in the NFL. So Jones decided to switch to wide receiver. At 6 feet 6 inches (1.98 m) tall, Jones had good size to be a wide receiver. Then he ran a 4.37-second 40-yard dash at the 2005 combine. Scouts were blown away by Jones's physical performance. The Jacksonville Jaguars ended up taking Jones in the first round of the draft. But he never became a star. Jones also struggled with off-field problems. He was out of the league after four seasons. It was a reminder

Quotable

"We've done a lot of mental conditioning and taken some practice tests to help us get acclimated and go in with a positive attitude. We've done a lot of basic things, like math, logic, and reading comprehension. But then there's been some other things that you haven't used in forever."

—Jonathan Cooper, describing part of his preparation for the 2013 NFL Scouting Combine. Cooper was an offensive tackle from the University of North Carolina. The Arizona Cardinals selected him in the first round of the 2013 NFL Draft.

Tennessee Titans running back Chris Johnson, *right*, has excelled in the NFL in part due to his great speed.

that football skills are more important than physical ability. Jerry Rice took a different path to the NFL. He played football at Mississippi Valley State University. That school

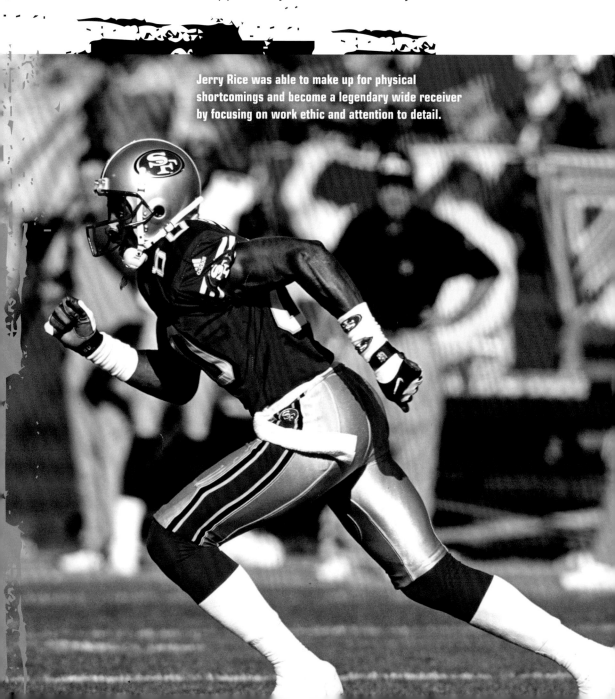

Jerry Rice was able to make up for physical shortcomings and become a legendary wide receiver by focusing on work ethic and attention to detail.

plays one level below the Division I level that most NFL players come from. As such, few regarded Rice as a top athlete like Jones. In fact, Rice's 4.6-second 40-yard dash was considered slow for a wide receiver. But Rice excelled in the NFL. He played most of his career with the San Francisco 49ers. Rice retired in 2004 holding every major record for his position. In 2010 the NFL Network named him the greatest player of all time.

"Football speed is how crisp you come out of running routes, how quickly you break off the line of scrimmage when the ball is snapped," Rice wrote in his book, *Go Long!* "The faster you can do all of these, the greater the advantage you have on the man covering you. Football speed can be learned through hard work and, after years of working on the track, I actually got faster as the years went on."

Speed is just one of many physical factors that teams consider when choosing players. They also look at skills such as balance, agility, endurance, strength, and vertical leap. In addition, teams value the mental tests and interviews at the combine. General managers want to find players who are highly skilled. But they also want players who have good character and who understand the game.

Character is important. NFL players face constant scrutiny from fans and coaches. They also earn a lot of money. These factors can lead to increased pressures from family, friends, and business partners. NFL teams want to make sure that players are mentally prepared for the NFL lifestyle.

IN THE SPOTLIGHT

Deion "Prime Time" Sanders was known for making a scene. That is what he did at the 1989 NFL Scouting Combine. The Florida State University cornerback blasted through the 40-yard dash in 4.27 seconds. And he just kept on running. He ran through the tunnel exiting the field at the Hoosier Dome in Indianapolis. He jogged outside to a waiting limousine. And he left for the airport.

Sanders did not want to participate in the 40-yard dash. Dallas Cowboys scouting director Gil Brandt said he persuaded Sanders to do so. Sanders went on to become a first-round pick in the draft. He was inducted into the Pro Football Hall of Fame in 2011. Sanders's speed made him a force on special teams as a kick returner. He returned 19 punts, kicks, interceptions, or fumbles for touchdowns in his career. That was an NFL record when he retired in 2005. Sanders also played wide receiver at times.

In addition, the interviews can offer insight into football matters. Players must be motivated and work well with teammates. They also must study the game and be able to understand what is happening. So teams might ask defensive players to break down an offensive play, for example. These interviews help give an idea of how players will adapt to the NFL.

CHAPTER THREE

LIFE IN THE

San Francisco 49ers tight end Vernon Davis is always fit. That was the case even when he was growing up. He ran the 40-yard dash in 4.45 seconds as a 16-year-old. He broke weight-lifting records as a freshman at the University of Maryland. Davis eventually reached 480 pounds (218 kg) in the bench press. And he squatted 685 pounds (311 kg) and had a 380-pound (172 kg) power clean lift. A power clean lift is when an athlete lifts a barbell to his shoulders.

Davis shined at the 2006 NFL Scouting Combine. He managed 33 repetitions of 225 pounds (102 kg) in the bench press. He also ran a 4.38-second 40-yard dash. Those were among the best performances ever by a tight end. The 49ers were certainly impressed. They selected Davis with the sixth overall pick in the 2006 NFL Draft.

San Francisco 49ers tight end Vernon Davis, left, uses his amazing strength and speed to get extra yards after a catch during a 2013 game.

NFL

Davis is a leader when it comes to fitness. But strength training is a necessity for all NFL players. Different positions require different types of strength. For example, defensive backs must be strong enough to tackle big receivers and running backs. Yet they also must maintain their quickness. Offensive linemen must be powerful and sturdy.

NFL teams have strength and conditioning coaches. These coaches help develop workout routines that fit each athlete's needs. Many players also have their own personal trainers. This is especially true in the off-season.

Davis coordinates his personal workouts with the 49ers' strength and conditioning coach.

"I'm just a competitive guy," Davis said. "I can't stand to see anyone do better than me. That's a part of competition. You've got to have that drive; that's how you get better. If a guy in front of me has a better bench press than me, I'm going to work harder to outdo him."

Not all workouts involve heavy lifting, though. NFL players and teams have adopted a number of different workout techniques. Some teams use yoga. The Seattle Seahawks use

Quotable

"In my first ten years in the NFL, our family never took a real vacation. Can you believe that? With the available time in the off-season and with our blessed financial situation, we could have traveled the world. But there was never a true off-season for me as I went right to work on my conditioning as soon as the season ended."
—Hall of Fame wide receiver Jerry Rice on the busy year-round schedules of NFL players

meditation sessions led by a sports psychologist. Detroit Lions running back Reggie Bush works out in something called Fre Flo Do. The workout takes place on a treadmill-like machine called the Launchpad. Bush dives over huge balls. He backpedals on the treadmill. He catches medicine balls thrown from above his head. Altogether, these drills provide an intense full-body workout.

Busy Schedules

NFL training camps begin in late July. The first regular-season games are in early September. There is little time off for players after that. Teams play one game per week. Usually games are on Sundays.

Dallas Cowboys running back Lance Dunbar does high-knee drills during training camp for the 2013 season.

However, the NFL also has games scheduled for Mondays, Thursdays, and some Saturdays. Players normally get just one day off each week during the season. They also have additional time off during their team's bye week.

The typical week is about more than just practicing. Players spend long hours at their team's facilities. They spend some of that time practicing or working out. But they also spend a lot of time in meetings. Teams break down video of the previous game. They prepare plans for the upcoming game. Players also spend a lot of time working with athletic trainers who help treat injuries.

Members of the Cleveland Browns stretch together before a game.

THOMPSON 51

FRYE 9

McKINLEY 97

ANDRUZZI 53

Physical activity is limited after a game. Players need that time to recover. They typically come in to the team facility on the Monday after a Sunday game. However, this day is mostly about watching video, going to team meetings, and recovering. NFL players sometimes refer to Monday as "sore day."

"You wake up the next day after a game and it's like you've been in several car crashes," former Philadelphia Eagles and Atlanta Falcons linebacker Ike Reese said. "You get in a car crash, even with your seat belt on, your body is going to ache. We're going full throttle into each other. A lot of times body size doesn't match. More weight, more force against you. Do that several times over three and a half hours and the next day you can't move."

Tuesday is typically an off day. Players are free to do what they want. However, most players still come in and watch film on their off day. Tuesday can be even worse for those still hurting from Sunday.

"Two days after the game was always the worst," former Tennessee Titans center Kevin Long said. "Just like with lifting. The first day after isn't the

Caught on Video

Most NFL games take place on Sundays. On Mondays, players and coaches watch video of the previous week's game. Make a mistake and it is likely to wind up on a big screen in the video room. The video of a game is broken down position by position. That allows coaches to point out the mistakes of individual players. It is there for everyone on the team to see. "Better hope you played well," former linebacker Jeremiah Trotter said.

worst. It's two days after that the injuries really start to stick out."

The longest practices are held the Wednesday and Thursday before a Sunday game. Players also study video of themselves and their next opponent during these days. A lighter practice is held Friday. For away games, teams usually travel on Saturday. They leave on Friday if it is a long trip. A light walk-through practice is held Saturday in the stadium where the game will be played.

Players are mostly on their own during the off-season. Many go back to their hometowns to be with friends and family and train. Others stay in town and work out at their team's facility. Either way, it is important that players stay in good shape. NFL training camps are very competitive. A player who shows up out of shape might be cut.

Teams also have a few official practices during the off-season. These are called minicamps or Organized Team Activities (OTAs). There may be up to six of these camps during the off-season. These events are opportunities for teams to check in on their players. Teams also use these camps to start planning for the upcoming season.

IN THE SPOTLIGHT

The Green Bay Packers' Clay Matthews is one of the NFL's toughest linebackers. The Packers selected him in the first round of the 2009 draft. He was named to the Pro Bowl in each of his first four years in the NFL.

Matthews credits training in mixed martial arts (MMA) as one of the reasons for his success. Several other NFL players also train in MMA. The goal of the training is to help athletes use their bodies in more aggressive ways. "In weightlifting, you have some time to relax, catch your breath, and then get after it with another set," Matthews said. "But with MMA, you have a guy that's pushing on you for a three- to five-minute round. It's always wearing on you so that mentally you have to push yourself beyond any place that you've been to before."

CHAPTER FOUR

THE NEED FOR FITNESS

Brett Favre spent 16 of his 20 NFL seasons as quarterback of the Green Bay Packers. He played in two Super Bowls and won one of them. He was the first quarterback in NFL history to pass for more than 70,000 yards. Hall of Fame quarterback and Fox Sports commentator Terry Bradshaw said Favre was the best player he has ever seen.

Favre retired after the 2010 season. He held many records at the time. The most famous mark might have been his iron man record. Favre started 297 consecutive games during his career. That streak lasted 19 seasons. Favre played through injuries during the streak. They ranged from a separated shoulder to a broken thumb. He had so many physical issues that he had personal trainers living with him at his home in Mississippi. Favre remembers one game when his ankle swelled. It was "six times its normal size and was badly discolored, an ugly shade of purple as I recall," he wrote in his book, *Favre*.

Quarterback Brett Favre was known as the NFL's iron man for his 297 consecutive games started, most of them with the Green Bay Packers.

AND NUTRITION

Mental toughness helped Favre keep his games-played streak going. However, an in-season and off-season training plan was important too. Favre established the routine during his high school and college years. Ken Croner is a performance specialist for the firm Athletes Performance. He was also Favre's personal trainer.

Croner lived in Favre's Mississippi house during the off-season before the 2007 season. He put Favre through workouts five days per week every week. They would be up at seven in the morning for the first workout session. Sometimes the workouts went into the night. Favre practiced with the local Oak Grove High School team three times per week. He would throw

Minnesota Vikings running back Adrian Peterson is known as one of the most physically fit players in the NFL.

passes to the team's receivers. He would also do sprints and run up the stadium stairs with the team.

"I admire Brett, how he plays and why he plays and his work ethic," Croner said. "The time and effort he put in was amazing. It really is."

One of the workouts that Croner initiated with Favre involved a bungee rope. He tied the rope to Favre's waist. The rope provided resistance. Favre then practiced a three-step drop. That is when a quarterback receives a snap and takes three steps back before making a pass. Then Favre would practice a four- or seven-step drop. Sometimes the bungee rope would be attached to both Favre and Croner as Favre practiced a rollout move. The drills helped Favre simulate game play.

Nutrition First

Physical training is only one part of staying healthy. NFL players also concentrate on nutrition both in season and out of season. Atlanta Falcons tight end Tony Gonzalez follows an 80/20 diet. The 80/20 diet consists of 80 percent plant-based food and 20 percent fish or chicken. Gonzalez eats food such as black bean burgers, oatmeal, salads, and rice. He also drinks vegan shakes and eats vegan organic chocolate chip cookies.

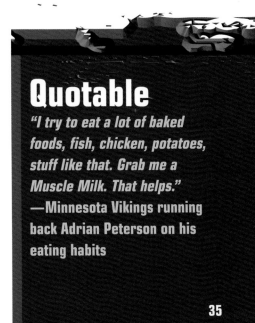

Quotable

"I try to eat a lot of baked foods, fish, chicken, potatoes, stuff like that. Grab me a Muscle Milk. That helps."
—Minnesota Vikings running back Adrian Peterson on his eating habits

Atlanta Falcons tight end Tony Gonzalez, *left*, hauls in a pass during a 2012 game.

"Let's say I catch five [passes] a game," Gonzalez said. "I get tackled five times. My body takes a pounding, no doubt. Why wouldn't I want to be putting healing stuff in my body?"

Houston Texans running back Arian Foster started a vegan diet in 2012. Some people wondered if he would get enough protein without eating meat. But Foster worked with a dietician to plan his diet. He said he started playing better after changing his eating habits.

Some players also use supplemental vitamins and pills. Fish oil supplements have become popular. New Orleans Saints quarterback Drew Brees uses Advocare Catalyst. This supplement provides an amino acid. The amino acid prevents muscles from breaking down.

Football players have many different roles, though. Skill position players such as Gonzalez and Foster must be quick and nimble. Linemen, however, need to be big. The Minnesota Vikings

Better Sleep

It is all about oxygen for Green Bay Packers linebacker A. J. Hawk. He had a new house built in 2006. And in his bedroom, Hawk had a hyperbaric oxygen therapy system installed. Three machines pump oxygen into his bedroom. The oxygen helps shorten the recovery time for Hawk after games and practices. "It's for endurance," Hawk said. "It was originally used by a lot of triathletes, distance runners, because it's supposed to increase your red blood cell count, help with recovery and endurance."

IN THE SPOTLIGHT

Football players are known for lifting weights and developing power. Many players have turned to a much more peaceful workout: yoga. Yoga is a spiritual discipline. Participants focus on breathing and meditation as they slowly go through a series of poses. Football players have found that yoga helps with flexibility and balance.

The New York Giants take yoga especially seriously. The team has employed a yoga instructor since 2004. Two of the Giants players who benefit from yoga are wide receiver Victor Cruz and quarterback Eli Manning. Those two players helped the Giants win Super Bowl XLVI after the 2011 season.

They are hardly alone. The Pittsburgh Steelers have used yoga since the 1990s. The Seattle Seahawks had optional yoga workouts in 2012. The workouts were so popular that the team made yoga mandatory in 2013.

selected left tackle Matt Kalil with the fourth pick in the 2012 NFL Draft. However, at 312 pounds (142 kg), the team worried he was undersized for his position. He had to eat upward of 7,000 calories per day to maintain his weight. Most people eat 2,000 or fewer calories daily. The food Kalil ate ranged from protein shakes to pasta to garlic bread to fresh vegetables.

CHAPTER FIVE

CONCUSSIONS AND

The NFL gridiron is a dangerous workplace. Injuries are common. Many players have careers shortened because of injuries. In 1985 Washington Redskins quarterback Joe Theismann was sacked. The play caused a compound fracture in Theismann's leg. He never played again. Mike Utley of the Detroit Lions became paralyzed following a play in a 1991 game. Michael Irvin, a receiver for the Dallas Cowboys, fell on his head while making a catch in a 1999 game. The fall ended his career.

Washington Redskins quarterback Robert Griffin III injures his knee while trying to grab a fumble during a playoff game in 2013.

FOOTBALL INJURIES

Broken bones, pulled muscles, and other injuries are a part of playing in the NFL. Edgeworth Economics studied NFL injuries from 2009 to 2012. It counted how many times an injury forced a player to sit out for at least eight days. There were 1,095 such instances in 2009. The number jumped to 1,496 in 2012. The NFL has responded to these types of studies by changing rules to reduce injuries. For example, the league found that kickoffs are particularly dangerous. The kicking team and the return team start far away from each other. By the time the players meet, they are moving very fast. These collisions cause a lot of injuries. So in 2011, the league moved kickoffs. The kicking team now starts at its own 35-yard line instead of the 30-yard line. Kicking from closer to the opposing team's end zone led to more touchbacks and fewer returns.

The NFL has also stepped up its efforts to prevent

A Better Future

Sean Morey is a retired wide receiver. He says he had several concussions during his 11-year NFL career. Now Morey is among nearly 200 NFL players who have committed to donating their bodies to research. When they die, the players will give their brains and spinal cord tissue to Boston University's Center for the Study of Traumatic Encephalopathy. The researchers hope to use their findings to better understand, prevent, and treat chronic traumatic encephalopathy (CTE). CTE is a degenerative disease that affects the brain. It is found in people with a history of repeated head trauma, including former NFL players. People suffering from CTE experience symptoms such as memory loss, aggression, depression, and dementia.

concussions. Concussions are brain injuries that occur when someone is hit in the head. Some concussions last only a few hours. Others can last a lifetime. The NFL has added new rules to try to limit concussions. For example, players are no longer allowed to initiate contact with the crowns of their helmets.

Trainers attend to Pittsburgh Steelers safety Shamarko Thomas after he was injured during a 2013 game.

"I think we've already seen a tremendous change in the way the game is played," said New York Giants safety Antrel Rolle. "I don't think it's going to go backwards. Players have already adapted to that style of play. We're trying to be more cautious of our tackling angling points."

Concussions are especially dangerous if players go back onto the field before they are fully healed. A second hit to the head can be deadly. That has not always stopped players, though. Many concussed players reenter games. They consider it a sign of toughness. The Associated Press (AP) surveyed 160 NFL players in 2010. It found that one-fifth of the players had hidden or "played down" concussion symptoms.

The NFL has been trying to change attitudes about concussions. The league educates players about brain-injury symptoms. Athletes are taught to alert medical trainers whenever they feel these symptoms. In addition, players can no longer return to a game or practice after experiencing concussion symptoms. The concussed players must sit out until their symptoms have gone away. Previously, players had to sit out of a game only if

Quotable

"We all understand the risk we take playing this game, but also down the road with our future health. I think that's part of the allure to the game is knowing you're putting your body in harm's way but understanding how much you love playing in a collision sport. Contact is a part of it. Our biggest fear as players, though, is not being able to walk off the field after an injury."
—Green Bay Packers quarterback Aaron Rodgers

they lost consciousness. One way doctors determine if a concussion has gone away is through baseline concussion tests. Players take these tests at the beginning of the season. The results show a player's normal characteristics. This helps show when a player is back to normal after a concussion.

Steve Young was a Super Bowl-winning quarterback for the San Francisco 49ers. However, his career ended in 1999 due to numerous concussions. He is happy that the NFL is now taking more precautions.

"The league is getting serious about it and they know that it is important," Young said. "Once you have a concussion, it is very hard to get back on the field."

The NFL is trying to limit concussions by penalizing helmet-to-helmet hits and other dangerous plays.

Aches and Pains

Major injuries and concussions can happen at any time. But for NFL players, minor injuries are a common reality. Players crash into one another at full speed on each play. Those collisions lead to constant aches and pains throughout the season.

Football has long had a warrior culture. Players are expected to be on the field as long as they are physically able. They are often willing to play through pain. Sometimes this is to show toughness. Other times players fear that sitting out will affect their chances of keeping their starting position. In extreme cases, players might even worry that they might lose their roster spot if they sit out. However, this desire to play through pain has led to a high use of painkillers. Former Chicago Bears star linebacker Brian Urlacher played 13 NFL seasons. He said he had 40 to 50 injections of a painkiller called Toradol during his career. He said some teammates took painkillers before every game.

Painkillers are dangerous. The drugs can have negative effects on one's liver and kidneys if taken in high amounts. Pain is the body's signal to stop. A player who does not feel pain might make his injuries worse. On top of all that, some painkillers can be addictive.

NFL players are encouraged to deal with their pain in safe ways. For example, they can take ice baths to reduce inflammation and pain. Teams also offer players sports massages and other treatments.

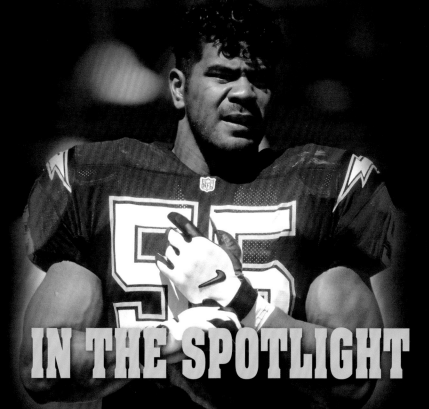

IN THE SPOTLIGHT

Junior Seau was a 12-time Pro Bowl player during his 20-year career. He was known as one of the toughest linebackers around. But friends and family members noticed he was behaving differently after retiring in 2010. He withdrew from those close to him. He made erratic decisions. He showed signs of depression. Then, in May 2012, he committed suicide.

The National Institutes of Health (NIH) studied Seau's brain. The brain showed abnormalities associated with CTE. It was noted that Seau had also shown symptoms common among those suffering from CTE.

The NIH study brought awareness to the issue of brain injuries. Afterward, the NFL agreed to spend millions of dollars on future research regarding concussions and head injuries. Seau's family claimed that the former player's condition came from repeated blows to the head during his football career. The claim was part of a suit brought against the NFL for concussion-related injuries. The NFL agreed to pay more than $700 million to more than 4,500 former players in 2013.

CHAPTER SIX

LEADERS ON

Expectations were low for University of Michigan quarterback Tom Brady. He was good in college. He was not the most skilled quarterback, though. Most figured he would struggle as a professional. So when the 2000 NFL Draft was held, Brady was not considered worthy of a high pick. Teams selected 198 players before the New England Patriots picked Brady in the sixth round. The Patriots were on to something.

New England Patriots quarterback Tom Brady, left, looks for an open receiver during Super Bowl XXXVI in 2002.

THE FIELD

Indianapolis Colts quarterback Andrew Luck, *No. 12*, directs his offense from the line of scrimmage before taking a snap in a 2013 game.

In just his second NFL season, Brady was named the MVP of Super Bowl XXXVI. He led the Patriots to a 20–17 victory over the St. Louis Rams. Brady was just 24. That made him the youngest quarterback at the time to win a Super Bowl. He then went on to win Super Bowls in two of the next three seasons.

The quarterback is usually considered the most important position in football. The quarterback is the leader of the offense. He touches the ball on almost every offensive play. Sometimes he hands it off to a running back. Sometimes he throws a pass. Sometimes he keeps the ball and runs with it. No matter who gets the ball on a given play, the quarterback is central to any football team.

A good quarterback can change an entire team's outlook. Brady began his NFL career on the scout team. Scout team players rarely become stars. Their job is simply to mimic the next opponent during practices. This helps the first-string players prepare for the opponent. Patriots

Quotable

"The thing about [Andrew] Luck is, that dude's not normal. I think just the type of player that he is, the guy stays calm all game long. Even if he throws interceptions or fumbles the ball, the guy steps into the pocket, he makes throws."
—Baltimore Ravens safety Bernard Pollard on quarterback Andrew Luck. Luck, then a rookie, led the Indianapolis Colts to the playoffs in 2012.

coach Bill Belichick saw something special in Brady, though.

"They'd go through the plays, and if somebody got something wrong, he'd correct them," Belichick said. "You could see them getting better."

Pregame Food Talk

Pregame rituals for some NFL players involve more than putting on their shoulder pads and getting taped up by the trainer. Former Chicago Bears middle linebacker Brian Urlacher had to eat two chocolate chip cookies before every game. Not one or three or four. Exactly two. St. Louis Rams quarterback Sam Bradford has a superstition too. He has to eat food in sets of three before a game. Often it is three pieces of fruit. "I have to have three pieces of cantaloupe, three pieces of pineapple. Everything in threes," Bradford said.

Brady was still the backup at the beginning of his second season. But starter Drew Bledsoe was injured in the second game. That is when Brady stepped in. He has been one of the NFL's best quarterbacks ever since.

Brady is not flashy. He does not run with the ball very often. Other quarterbacks have stronger arms. But Brady is confident in the pocket. When he drops back to pass, teammates know the pass will be accurate. They trust him to make plays, and he usually does.

"To me, he's the best quarterback in the league, and he's done it for a long time," said Pittsburgh Steelers quarterback Ben Roethlisberger, who has won two Super Bowls himself.

Other Positions

What makes Brady stand out is his consistency and leadership. The Patriots are known for letting star players leave to join other teams. Brady is the one constant. The team trusts him to always be prepared and play at a high level. This preparation and leadership help elevate the players around him.

A quarterback cannot win by himself, though. NFL teams have 11 players on the field at a time. Each

New Orleans Saints quarterback Drew Brees, *left*, is one of the most prolific passers in NFL history.

player has a specific job. Wide receivers run routes, catch passes, and sometimes are called on to block. Offensive linemen block pass rushers and create holes for running backs to go through. Defensive backs must tightly cover

receivers and not let running backs break free. Kickers handle kickoffs and field goal attempts. A punter's job is solely to punt.

Safety Troy Polamalu has long been a leader on the Pittsburgh Steelers' defense.

There is no quarterback on defense. Sometimes free safeties assume a similar role as leader of a defense. However, the middle linebacker is most often that leader. The middle linebacker is positioned at the center of the defense. He plays a key role on almost every play. On running plays, the middle linebacker rushes forward to try to tackle the runner. On passing plays, he often drops into pass coverage. Sometimes he might blitz and try to sack the quarterback. The middle linebacker often gets play calls from the coaches and relays the information to his teammates.

Ray Lewis was one of the best middle linebackers ever. He was strong and played physically. But he was also smart. He knew just where to be. He was also a good leader. Lewis set the tone for the entire Baltimore Ravens defense. And it was no coincidence that Baltimore

Formations

Each football team has 11 players on the field at a time. However, teams use many different combinations. An offense always has five linemen and a quarterback. A standard offense uses two wide receivers, a tight end, a running back, and a fullback. But teams might use as many as five wide receivers on a given play. Defenses are even more versatile. NFL teams play with a 3–4 or 4–3 defense. Those numbers refer to how many linemen and linebackers are on the field. A 3–4 defense uses four linebackers. That allows teams to get more creative with blitzes but puts more pressure on the linemen. Another formation is called nickel. This involves a fifth defensive back replacing a linebacker. The nickel formation is common on third downs when the opposing offense is likely to pass.

often had one of the best defenses during Lewis's career. Lewis retired after the 2012 season. But it was not before he led the Ravens to a second Super Bowl title.

"How could it end any other way than that? And now I get to ride into the sunset with my second [Super Bowl] ring," Lewis said.

IN THE SPOTLIGHT

Matt Prater has three jobs each Sunday. One job is kicking off. The other jobs are similar: attempting field goals and extra points. Prater gets on the field only for those special teams plays. The Denver Broncos expect him to perform well in those situations.

One way in which Prater practices field goals is by kicking through narrow goalposts. In NFL and college games, the goalposts are 18 feet 6 inches (5.64 m) apart. In practice, Prater often kicks through uprights that are just 8.5 feet (2.59 m) apart.

"Kicking on the skinny uprights for so long, when I got back to the regular ones, my line up just looks a lot wider, so I'm more confident when I kick," Prater said.

The narrow practice goalposts have paid off for Prater. The Broncos' kicker made a 64-yard field goal in 2013. That was an NFL record.

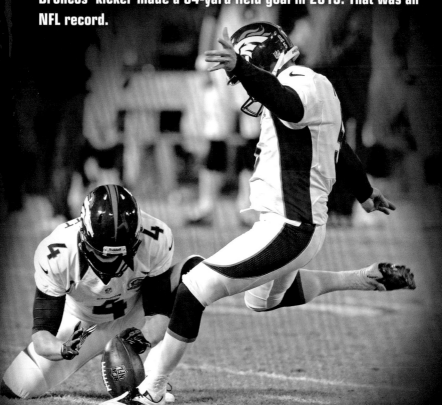

Train Like a Pro

Nothing beats speed in the NFL. Here are three training drills that help make an athlete faster. They were developed and used by former Jacksonville Jaguars and Miami Dolphins defensive back Donovin Darius. He now operates Donovin Darius Next Level Training and Performance. He is based in Florida but travels to different cities to host camps.

Arms

Assume a standing position in front of a mirror with your feet a shoulder width apart. Bend your elbows at 90 degrees and have the palms of your hands facing each other. Bring one arm up so that your hand is in front of you. At the same time, your other arm goes down so that your hand is near your hips. While standing, pump your arms quickly for 20 seconds at a time. Do not move anything but your arms. Start out by doing the exercise five times with one minute between each 20-second set.

Feet

This exercise also takes place in front of a mirror. Stand tall. Put your arms in the position learned in the last exercise. Then run as fast as you can in place. Bring your knees up halfway. Keep them positioned forward. Do not let your heels touch the ground. Darius says this is a drill that can help "teach your muscles and nerves to fire fast while you are working on perfect form running." This exercise also can be done for 20 seconds at a time with a rest period of one minute between each set.

Knees

In this drill, you should take the same position in front of a mirror and run in place just as you did in the feet exercise. But this time bring your knees up to your hips when running in place. Darius says this exercise helps your core and leg muscles develop strength and endurance. Perform the drill for 20 seconds at a time with one minute of rest between sets.

Football Gear Diagram

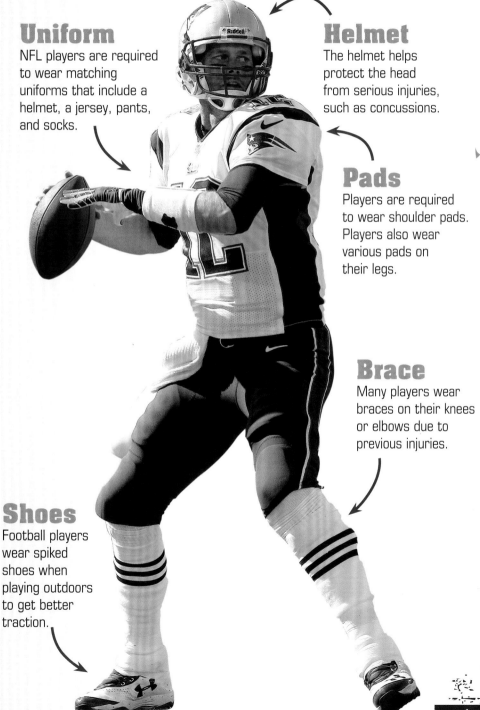

Uniform
NFL players are required to wear matching uniforms that include a helmet, a jersey, pants, and socks.

Helmet
The helmet helps protect the head from serious injuries, such as concussions.

Pads
Players are required to wear shoulder pads. Players also wear various pads on their legs.

Brace
Many players wear braces on their knees or elbows due to previous injuries.

Shoes
Football players wear spiked shoes when playing outdoors to get better traction.

Glossary

bye: an off week

concussion: a brain injury that occurs when something jolts a person's head

degenerative: something that gets worse and worse

diet: a person's regular food intake

merge: when two things join together as one

minicamp: shortened versions of preseason camps. Many teams have three- or four-day camps during the off-season for rookies and mandatory minicamps for returning players.

pocket: the area between the offensive tackles

psychological test: an examination that tests the mental capacity of a player. It reveals the personality of a person and what he or she would do in certain situations.

rookie: a first-year NFL player

salary: the amount of money that is paid to a person for their work

shuttle: agility tests that involve moving between two places multiple times as quickly as possible

special teams: the units on a football team that play during field goals, kickoffs, and punts

touchback: a play when a player receives a punt, kick, or turnover in his own end zone and downs the ball. The team then gets the ball at the 20-yard line.

vegan: a diet that avoids any animal products, including meat and dairy

For More Information

Der, Bob, ed. *Sports Illustrated Kids Big Book of Who: Football*. New York: Time Home Entertainment, 2013.
This book highlights some of the biggest stars in the NFL, both past and present.

Fox Sports NFL
http://www.foxsports.com/nfl
This website has lots of news and information about the NFL and its players.

Kennedy, Mike, and Mark Stewart. *Touchdown: The Power and Precision of Football's Perfect Play*. Minneapolis: Millbrook Press, 2010.
Learn everything one could possibly want to know about football's most exciting play, the touchdown.

National Football League
http://www.nfl.com
Visit this website to discover all things about the NFL, including history, teams, players, and records.

NFL Scouting Combine
http://www.nflcombine.net
Visit this website to find dates, news, and information about the annual NFL Scouting Combine. Included are some of the records that have been set at the combine sessions.

Savage, Jeff. *Aaron Rodgers*. Minneapolis: Lerner Publications, 2012.
Learn about Green Bay Packers superstar quarterback Aaron Rodgers in this biography.

Source Notes

6   Peyton Manning, *Manning* (New York: HarperCollins Publishers, 2000), 85.

18   Brett Friedlander, "Cooper Ready to Show Off His Skills at NFL Scouting Combine," Wilmington (NC) *Star News Online*, February 20, 2013, http://acc.blogs.starnewsonline.com/35160 /cooper-ready-to-show-off-his-skills-at-nfl-scouting-combine/.

21   Jerry Rice, *Go Long!* (New York: Ballantine Books, 2007), 35.

26   Joe Wuebben, "Super Bowl Spotlight: Vernon Davis," *Muscle & Fitness*, accessed January 15, 2014, http://www .muscleandfitness.com/workouts/athletes-and-celebrities /super-bowl-spotlight-vernon-davis.

26   Rice, *Go Long!*, 99.

29   Anthony L. Gargano, *NFL Unplugged* (Hoboken, NJ: John Wiley & Sons, 2010), 194.

29   Ibid., 199.

29–30   Ibid., 195.

31   Sam Farmer, "Mixed Martial Arts Helps NFL Players Improve Skills and Deal with Lockout," *Los Angeles Times*, June 6, 2011, http://articles.latimes.com/2011/jun/06/sports /la-sp-farmer-nfl-20110607.

33   Brett Favre and Bonita Favre, *Favre* (New York: Rugged Land, 2004), 110.

35   Tom Silverstein and Bob McGinn, "Workouts Paying Off for Favre," *Milwaukee Journal Sentinel*, August 2, 2007, http://www.jsonline .com/sports/packers/29262134.html.

35   Scott Neumyer, "The 25 Fittest Football Players," *Men's Fitness*, August 1, 2012, http://www.mensfitness.com/leisure/sports /the-25-fittest-football-players.

37   Kevin Gray, "Going Vegan in the NFL," *Men's Journal*, December 2012, http://www.mensjournal.com/magazine /going-vegan-in-the-nfl-20130123.

37   Lori Nickel and Tom Silverstein, "Well-Conditioned Machine," *Milwaukee Journal Sentinel*, November 10, 2006, http://www .jsonline.com/sports/packers/29181689.html.

44 Judy Battista, "NFL Won't Drop Player Safety after Concussion Lawsuit Settlement," *NFL*, September 3, 2013, http://www.nfl .com/news/story/0ap1000000237695/article/nfl-wont-drop -player-safety-after-concussion-lawsuit-settlement.

44 "New NFL Concussion Rules Take Effect," *CBSNews*, December 3, 2009, http://www.cbsnews.com/news/new-nfl-concussion-rules -take-effect/.

44 C. J., "C. J.: Greg Jennings Going Huggy Bear on Aaron Rodgers Didn't Heal Rift," Minneapolis *Star Tribune*, October 30, 2013, http://www.startribune.com/entertainment/229945841 .html?page=2&c=y.

45 Mike Sorensen, "Steve Young Speaks with Deseret News about Concussions in Football," *Deseret News* (Salt Lake City), June 25, 2012, http://www.deseretnews.com/article/765585877 /Steve-Young-speaks-with-Deseret-News-about-concussions-in -football.html.

51 Edward Lee, "Still a Rookie, QB Andrew Luck a Big Part of Colts' Success," *Baltimore Sun*, January 5, 2013, http://articles .baltimoresun.com/2013-01-05/sports/bs-sp-ravens-colts -andrew-luck-0106-20130105_1_andrew-luck-ravens-offensive -coordinator-ravens-cornerback-cary-williams.

52 Charles P. Pierce, *Moving the Chains* (New York: Farrar, Straus and Giroux, 2006), 10.

52 Will Brinson, "Ben Roethlisberger: Tom Brady Still 'Best Quarterback in the League,'" *CBSSports.com*, October 30, 2013, http://www.cbssports.com/nfl/eye-on-football/24161912/ben -roethlisberger-tom-brady-still-best-quarterback-in-the-league.

52 101espn, "Sam Bradford on His Ping Pong Table and Pregame Rituals-101ESPN," *YouTube*, last modified January 4, 2011, https://www.youtube.com/watch?v=QWjwi41yYXc.

56 Associated Press, "Ray Lewis Ends Career with Title," *ESPN*, February 4, 2013, http://espn.go.com/nfl/playoffs/2012/story /_/id/8912407/.

57 Arnie Stapleton, Associated Press, "Some Kickers Using Narrower Goal Posts at Practice." *Minnesota Vikings*, December 31, 2009, http://www.vikings.com/news/article-1/Some-Kickers -Using-Narrower-Goal-Posts-At-Practice/3e75fc9b-9a51-4841 -886e-b65a94c151e1.

Index

About the Author

Paul D. Bowker is a freelance writer and author based in Chesterton, Indiana. He has authored five other sports books for young readers. He is also a high school soccer official licensed in three states. Bowker is national past president of Associated Press Sports Editors, and has won several national and state writing awards. He lives with his wife and daughter.

Photo Acknowledgments

The images in this book are used with the permission of: © Rich Gabrielson/Icon SMI, pp. 3 (top), 4–5; © Ray Carlin/Icon SMI, pp. 3 (middle), 13, 34; © Ric Tapia/Icon SMI, pp. 3 (bottom), 38, 45, 57; © Zuma Press/Icon SMI, pp. 7, 36–37, 40–41, 53; © Chicago Daily News, Inc./Library of Congress, pp. 8–9; © NFL Photos/AP Images, p. 10; © John Pyle/Icon SMI, pp. 14–15; © Cliff Welch/Icon SMI, p. 16; © TMB/Icon SMI, pp. 18–19; © John McDonough/Icon SMI, p. 20; © Icon Sports Media, p. 22; © Joe Toth/BPI/Icon SMI, pp. 24–25; © Adam Davis/Icon SMI, p. 27; © Jerry Sharp/Shutterstock Images, p. 28; © Jeff Lewis/Icon SMI, p. 31; © Allen Fredrickson/Icon SMI, pp. 32–33; © Kellen Micah/Icon SMI, pp. 43, 54; © John Cordes/Icon SMI, p. 47; © John Biever/Icon SMI, pp. 48–49; © Zach Bolinger/Icon SMI, pp. 50–51; © Richard A. Brightly/Icon SMI, p. 59.

Front cover: © Ron Antonelli/Getty Images; © Valentina Razumova/Shutterstock.com, (stadium lights).

Main body text set in Eurostile LT Pro 12/18. Typeface provided by Linotype.